Liberty Beautiful Hair

Written by Yvette Daniels
Words edited by Melissa Colgan
Words edited by Shelia Y. Darden

Illustrated by: Tooba Imtiaz

All rights reserved. International copyright secured. No parts of this book may be reproduced or transmitted in any form or by any means, electronic or mechanical, including photocopying, recording or by any information stored in a retrieving system, without permission in writing from the owner.

For Information regarding Permission – Email: victoriousfruit@hotmail.com

Victorious Fruit Music Studio © 2013

This Book Belongs to:

_____

My name is Liberty. I used to be unhappy with my hair. Every morning, before I would start my day, I would look in the mirror and I would get so upset when I looked at my hair.

It is thick, curly, and hard to comb. When it is hot and humid outside, my hair sweats and gets tangled. My momma would use a thick comb to get it untangled and I would cry and say, "It hurts momma, please stop. I do not like this hair, I do not like this hair."

Until one day my momma sat me down to talk to me. As she combed and brushed my hair, she shared a story to remind me who I am.

"Liberty, you are so beautiful, " said Momma, "God made you perfect in His eyes. God said you are Fearfully and Wonderfully made. God created all things to be Beautiful. He gave you just what you needed."

Momma said, "Sometimes we are not happy with what we have, and we tend to look at what someone else has, and not realize what we have is special, and that includes our beautiful hair."

Liberty said, "I just get tired of my hair, and I get tired of people making fun of my hair especially when it is all tangled and curly."

"Liberty," said Momma, "You and your hair with all its unique styles is what makes the world beautiful. We are all different. We are all different colors, different sizes, different races, and different cultures. If everyone looks the same, there will be no true beauty in the world."

Momma: "Do you know why I named you Liberty?"

Liberty: "No momma, why did you name me Liberty?"

"Liberty means Freedom - you are free to be who you want to be. "You are not meant to have hair like anyone else. You should love your hair because God created you and designed you as you are. The best part of your hair is you can wear your hair in many different hair styles."

When momma finished combing and brushing Liberty's hair, Momma gave Liberty a handheld mirror.
Liberty looked in the mirror and stood up. Liberty said,
"I look so beautiful."

Momma: "remember what I told you, Liberty, that you can wear your hair in many different hair styles."

You can wear curly hair.
You can wear braids.
You can wear big twists.

You can wear a big afro.
You can wear French braids.
You can wear a little afro.

You can wear straight hair.
You can wear a ponytail.
You can wear your hair in a bun.
You just have beautiful hair!

Liberty: "this is why I love my hair – just the way God made it!"

Dear Princess

I formed you in your Mother's belly.
I was so excited to create you.
I created you in my own image.
Your face, your eyes, your nose, your mouth, your ears,
your hair, your arms, your legs.
I created you from head to toe.
When I created you, nobody was on my mind - But You!
I put gifts and talents in you.
To bring Glory and Honor to my Name.
You are so beautiful! You are my creation, saith the Lord.
When I created you, I made your hair just right.
When I created you, I made your color just right.
When I created you, I made your height just right.
When I created you, I made your shape just right.
When I created you, I said that is Very Good!
As you grow, remember God is your Creator and no one else.
Do not allow people to talk about you or put
you down - that's an insult to me.

When you look into the mirror, what do you see?
I see a beautiful Girl created by me!
Love God

By Yvette Daniels

About the Author

Yvette Daniels comes from a large family of Singers and Musicians. She is a Musician, Music Teacher, and Minister of Worship at her church. Yvette has been teaching music for over 20 years. She arranges music for her Church's Orchestra and writes Children's Choir Songs and Praise & Worship Songs. Yvette has published 6 Children's Books and 6 Coloring and Activity Books. She has also published a Christian Book – Breaking Free (Freedom From the Snares). Yvette is currently in the process of completing 2 more Children's Books and a Songbook.

CHILDREN BOOKS AVAILABLE BY
YVETTE DANIELS
Amazon & Barnes & Nobles

Harry, Harry, the Dancing Hippo
Ten Singing Cockatiels
Dance, Jump, Hop and Sing
The Music on the Bus
Sweet Pea Paw Prints
Unicorn Coloring Book
African American Magic Coloring Book
African American Black Girls Coloring Book
Monster Truck Coloring Book
Animal Dot to Dot Coloring Book

Email: victoriousfruit@hotmail.com

Seven Little Mice Chasing Waves
Bubbles the Goldfish Coloring and Activity Book
Breaking Free (Freedom From the Snare)

www.ingramcontent.com/pod-product-compliance
Lightning Source LLC
Chambersburg PA
CBHW041106070526
44583CB00002B/82